How to Read a Recipe

BY ANITRA BUDD

The Child's World®
childsworld.com

Published by The Child's World®
1980 Lookout Drive • Mankato, MN 56003-1705
800-599-READ • www.childsworld.com

Photographs ©: Zen Fruit Graphics/Shutterstock Images, cover (foreground); Vasilyeva Larisa/Shutterstock Images, cover (background), 3, 23; Wong Yu Liang/Shutterstock Images, 5; iStockphoto, 6, 7, 9, 17; Shutterstock Images, 11 (background), 19; Robyn Mackenzie/Shutterstock Images, 11 (foreground); Natalia Lebedinskaia/Shutterstock Images, 13; Iakov Filimonov/Shutterstock Images, 15; Stafford Studios/iStockphoto, 16; Red Line Editorial, 18

ISBN 9781503823303
LCCN 2017944890

Printed in the United States of America
PA02360

ABOUT THE AUTHOR

Anitra Budd is a writer and editor. She enjoys reading, sewing, and baking. She lives in Minneapolis, Minnesota, with her family.

Table of Contents

CHAPTER 1

A Recipe for Fun

Picture your favorite food. Do you know what is in it? Do you know how it is made? You would if you knew the recipe.

Recipes tell people how to make food and drinks. There are recipes for all kinds of foods, from pies and pasta to sandwiches and soup. Recipes have been around a long time. Some of the oldest recipes are almost 4,000 years old.

Some families write their own recipes. If they have lots of recipes, they might put them in a book. Books with many recipes are called cookbooks.

Reading recipes teaches you how to follow instructions. It is also a good way to practice math and reading.

Many families enjoy cooking together.

Cooking can be lots of fun. Cooks are like artists. Their food is their art. When you cook, you can make tasty treats to share. Knowing how to read a recipe is the first step to cooking.

Once you know how to read recipes, you can write your own. Test **ingredients** and write down **directions**. Make up funny names for your new dishes. Pretty soon, you might have enough recipes for your own cookbook!

Cookbooks can have many different recipes.

Recipes allow you to experiment with food.

7

CHAPTER 2

Recipe Basics

Recipes can look very different. There is no one way to write a recipe. Still, most recipes have the same main parts.

Title

Every recipe has a title, like "Sunshine Eggs" or "Blueberry Banana Muffins." The title often tells you the main ingredients or flavors in the dish.

Ingredients

Ingredients are what goes into the dish. Milk, salt, and flour are common ingredients. Ingredients are usually listed in the order you will use them.

Fresh ingredients give dishes flavor.

The ingredients list also gives **measurements**. Measurements tell you how much of an ingredient to use. For example, "2 tablespoons" and "2 cups" are both measurements.

Servings are the number of people a recipe will feed. If a recipe says it makes five servings, it makes enough for five people.

Servings are only a guess. A five-serving recipe may feed only three very hungry people. Or it might make enough for eight people who are not so hungry.

Directions

The steps to make a dish are called directions. A recipe direction for a cake might say, "Mix batter well." The directions might describe what the food should look like. A cookie recipe might say, "Bake until golden brown."

The directions list steps in order. That is why it is important to read them from beginning to end.

 Title

Ants on a Log

Ingredients:

1 large celery stalk

4 tablespoons peanut butter

2 tablespoons raisins

Makes 2 servings

 Servings

Directions:

1. Rinse the celery.

2. With a grown-up's help, cut the celery stalk into four pieces.

3. Spread peanut butter on the celery sticks.

4. Place raisins in rows on the peanut butter.

5. Enjoy!

11

How to Read a Recipe

First, read the recipe slowly so that you understand the directions. Some recipes have pictures to show the steps. Look at these carefully.

Clean Hands

Wash your hands before you touch any food. Dirty hands spread germs. Some germs can make people sick. When you cook, wash your hands every time you:

- touch your face or hair.
- use the bathroom.
- touch raw eggs or meat.
- sneeze.
- blow your nose.

It is important to wash your hands before cooking.

13

Ingredients and Tools

Next, get the ingredients. The ingredients list might tell you to **prepare** ingredients. Peeling and mashing are two common ways to prepare ingredients.

The ingredients list can be tricky. For example, "1 cup chopped walnuts" is not the same as "1 cup walnuts, chopped." Why? The first means you should chop, *then* measure the walnuts. The second means you should measure the walnuts, *then* chop them.

Get your spoons, bowls, and other tools ready. If you need to use an oven or a knife, ask a grown-up to help.

Reading directions slowly will help you make sure you don't miss a step.

Follow the Steps

Follow the directions in order. If you do not, the recipe will not work. Say the directions out loud so you do not miss a step.

Recipe Abbreviations

Many recipes use **abbreviations**. An abbreviation is a short form of a word. For example, "Oct." is an abbreviation for "October."

Measurements in recipes are often abbreviated.

Recipes help people try new foods.

Recipes use abbreviations for measurements. On the next page, you will find the most common measurement abbreviations.

MEASUREMENT ABBREVIATIONS

teaspoon	t or tsp
tablespoon	T or Tbsp
cup	c or C
ounce	oz
pint	pt
quart	qt
gallon	gal
pound	lb or #
package	pkg

Some cookbooks use different abbreviations in their recipes. Abbreviations and their meanings will usually be listed in the front or the back of the book.

Now that you have all the tools you need to read a recipe, it is time to start cooking! What kinds of foods will you make?

Recipes are often shared with family and friends.

1. How old are some of the oldest recipes?

    A. 300 years

    B. 500 years

    C. 2,000 years

    D. 4,000 years

2. What is an abbreviation?

3. Which is an abbreviation for "cup"?
- A. CP
- B. C
- C. c/p
- D. C.P.

4. What can you learn from a recipe title?

GLOSSARY

abbreviations (uh-bree-vee-AY-shunz) Abbreviations are short forms of words. "T" or "Tbsp" are abbreviations for "tablespoon."

directions (duh-REK-shuns) Directions are instructions on how to do something. Recipe directions tell you how to make a dish.

ingredients (in-GREE-dee-ents) Ingredients are parts of a mixture. Flour and water are ingredients in bread.

measurements (MEH-zhur-mentz) Measurements are an amount of something. "One cup" and "2 teaspoons" are both recipe measurements.

prepare (pree-PAYR) To prepare means to get ready. You can prepare carrots by peeling them.

servings (SIR-vingz) Servings are helpings of food or drink. Recipes can make one or more servings.

TO LEARN MORE

In the Library

Better Homes and Gardens. *New Junior Cookbook.* Hoboken, NJ: Wiley, 2012.

Hussain, Nadiya. *Nadiya's Bake Me a Story.* London, UK: Hachette Children's Books, 2016.

Kid Chef Eliana. *Cool Kids Cook: Fresh and Fit.* Gretna, LA: Pelican Publishing Company, 2014.

On the Web

Visit our Web site for links about how to read a recipe:

childsworld.com/links

Note to Parents, Teachers, and Librarians: We routinely verify our Web links to make sure they are safe and active sites. So encourage your readers to check them out!

INDEX

ANSWER KEY

1. **How old are some of the oldest recipes?** D. 4,000 years

2. **What is an abbreviation?** An abbreviation is a shorter form of a word or a group of words.

3. **Which is an abbreviation for "cup"?** B. C

4. **What can you learn from a recipe title?** A recipe's title may tell you the main ingredients or flavors in the dish.